2-5-22

Helicopters, Drill Sergeants, and Consultants

Jim Fay

Parenting Styles and the Messages They Send

Library of Congress Catalog Card Number: 94-76328

ISBN 0-944634-03-6

Printed in the United States of America

Illustrations by
Paule Niedrach Botkin

Introduction

I have two addictions—kids and psychology.

It's pretty easy to figure out why I grew addicted to kids, but with psychology it's less obvious. I became addicted to psychology because I grew up learning how to use power, and I finally got tired of fighting with everybody.

I had a good model to teach me how to use power—my dad. He used to say, "I don't care how you feel about it. I want it done now!"

I said, "Yes, sir!" Then I jumped up and did it right then.

He talked to my mother the same way. He said, "I don't care if those kids love me or not. I expect them to grow up, be responsible, and do what I tell them to do. It's your job to get it done."

Mom used to say, "Yes, sir!" too.

When I grew up, I tried a number of occupations. I traveled as a professional musician. I worked as a lumberjack. Finally, I became a teacher.

What do you think were my first words in the classroom? "I don't care how you feel about it. I want it done now!"

After many years as a teacher and school administrator, I'm going to suggest that you try not using power with your children.

In place of power, I'm suggesting some practical and usable tools for parents and teachers that are adapted from formal psychological concepts.

I offer them as suggestions. You may chew on all of them, and you don't have to swallow a single one of them whole. I'm not trying to make you feel guilty. I'm not trying to tell you what you're doing wrong with your children.

I simply want to share some psychological techniques that raised the quality of my life dramatically. I also want to do this because, for me, sharing these ideas is fun!

Jim Fay

Parenting Styles, Love and Logic

Helicopters, drill sergeants, and consultants are analogies I use to identify three different parenting styles.

Most parents deal with their children in one of these three styles.

Some parents hover over their children like helicopters, constantly rescuing them and constantly protecting them from their teachers, other kids, and the rest of the cruel world out there.

Some parents are like drill sergeants. They say, "When I tell you to jump, you jump."

And some parents are like consultants. They're always willing to share alternatives. They're always willing to describe how they would solve the problem themselves (if it were their problem).

And they're always saying, "It's not my life. You get to decide. And good luck to you." Then consultant parents always hold kids responsible and accountable for their decisions.

With their distinct parenting styles, helicopters, drill sergeants, and consultants send different unspoken messages to their children.

A helicopter's message is, "You can't help yourself. I have to do things for you."

A drill sergeant implies, "You can't think. I have to do your thinking for you."

A consultant parent's unspoken message is, "You're capable and can make wise decisions. You are a responsible person"

In the pages that follow we'll meet all three types of parents, and we'll see some events in their lives. As we chuckle about their stories, we may also see ourselves and our children in both their problems and in the solutions they find.

The solutions parents find in these stories come from using techniques based on a philosophy I developed with my good friend, Foster W. Cline, M.D. This philosophy is called Love and Logic.

Love allows children to grow through their mistakes. Logic allows them to live with the consequences of their choices. The solutions offered through Love and Logic are based on these four principles:

1. Shared control—Parents gain control by giving away the control they don't need.

2. Shared thinking and decision-making—Parents provide opportunities for children to do the greatest amount of thinking and decision-making.

3. Equal shares of consequences and empathy—An absence of parental anger causes a child to think and learn from his or her mistakes.

4. Maintaining a child's self-concept—Improved self-concept leads to improved behavior and improved achievement.

Drill sergeants tend to avoid giving children opportunities to make decisions—or mistakes. Helicopters tend to rescue kids from the consequences of their actions. Consultant parents, however, allow kids to make mistakes and to live with the consequences.

But, instead of explaining and theorizing, let's meet some parents and kids. As you read their stories and see their dilemmas, I'm sure you'll begin to grasp what Love and Logic parenting is all about.

Hovering and Rescuing

Helicopters make a lot of noise, a lot of wind, a lot of racket. Helicopters hover, they protect, and they rescue.

Helicopter parents are easy to recognize. They're the parents going in and out of the school's front doors each morning carrying coats, lunches, violins, papers . . .

As a school principal I used to watch these parents in awe and ask myself, "Gee, how did those children ever train their parents to do that?"

I have a good friend, Robert, who's a superb helicopter. His story gave me the answer to that question.

With Robert's first daughter, Lisa, he and his wife were superb helicopters.

When Lisa was born, he said, "I'm going to be the best daddy who ever lived. I want to show her she is loved because I want her to love herself and take care of herself."

"To do that I'm going to make all the sacrifices needed."

He and his wife never went anywhere without Lisa. Do you have any idea how hard it is to roll a bowling ball with a child tucked under your arm? That's about how bad it was!

Pretty soon the couple felt as if they were drowning in parenthood. It was no fun. They needed some time alone. Robert went to Lisa and said, "Lisa, Mom and I need some time alone. There's going to be a baby-sitter tonight. She's coming at 7:30."

Lisa said, "I don't want a baby-sitter. I want you home with me."

They said, "She's a nice lady."

Lisa cried.

Robert and his wife canceled the baby-sitter.

They told themselves, "That's okay. We'll make those sacrifices. She will know she is loved, she will love herself, and she will grow up to take good care of herself."

Wrong. It doesn't work that way.

In kindergarten a classmate who had forgotten her mittens asked to borrow Lisa's. Lisa couldn't say no. At recess Lisa was out building a snowman with her bare hands.

In fourth grade Lisa was in charge of snacks for her Brownie troop—every meeting.

At sixteen, Lisa was a nice young teenager—but she let everyone else meet their own needs at her expense.

She couldn't stand that forever. Sooner or later she was bound to get mad, and when she did, she was no longer fun to be around.

Robert asked a psychiatrist friend, "What's wrong?"

He answered, "Nothing. You programmed her that way."

And they had.

You see, when helicopter parents hover, they focus so intensely on the needs of their child that they ignore their own needs. Even as they hover they are modeling doormat behavior.

Kids never learn from being told; they learn from being shown. Lisa had learned what her parents had shown her.

Helicopter parents are also great rescuers.

When Johnny comes home from school, droops over the kitchen table, and moans, "I don't have any friends," helicopter parents rev up their motors and the racket begins.

"No, friends? That's serious. What is your teacher doing about that anyway? Nothing? That figures! Do they ever change the seats around so that you can sit with other kids and show what a good friend you can be? Do they ever tell other kids to be nice to you? Does your teacher ever tell the kids that you need friends? Don't worry. I'm going over to see the principal tomorrow. Some things are going to change over there."

(After a brief pause for breath, the whirring continues.)

"Come to think of it, I haven't seen very many kids here on weekends, so you can show them what a wonderful friend you can be. You pick out three kids, and while you're at school tomorrow I'll call their parents so they can spend the night here this weekend. Don't worry, honey, we'll get this fixed for you."

If you listen very hard, under all that racket you can hear a very quiet—and very powerful—implied message.

You see, the most powerful messages in the world have nothing at all to do with the words being said.

Let's leave the helicopter pad briefly to look at implied messages.

If you listen closely you will hear the implied messages in these common parental comments:

"Your sister was in that class last year, and she did so well."
Am I talking about the sister? No way!

"What are you doing that for?"
Sounds like a question, but it's not. I'm not really asking her to describe why she's doing that.

"How old are you?"
Has the parent really forgotten the age of the child?

"If I've told you once, I've told you a thousand times."

"What grade did you say you're in?"

Not one of these messages means anything like the real words. Every one of them has an implied message, a put-down that says,

"You're not good enough."

"You don't think for yourself."

"You're acting like a baby."

"You don't listen."

"You're not learning fast enough."

The put-down is not in the actual words, but lies beneath them in the tone and voice inflection. I can send implied put-downs with the world's most loving words.

"Now, honey, you're not going out without your coat on today."

What's the implied message? "I don't think you're smart enough to know whether you'll be hot or cold."

Then there's the inevitable question from the front seat of the car . . . "Kiddo, are you sure you need to go to the bathroom? You just went ten minutes ago."

What's implied? "You're so fuzzy-headed, you don't even know when your body functions are going to work. I'll determine your needs."

If the implied message is so devastating, why do we send it?

Do we hate kids?

Do we want them to hate us?

Do we want them to be miserable around us?

Do we want them to grow up and feel miserable about themselves?

No, of course not. We say these things because these phrases are locked in unconsciously from our childhood. And we've heard and used them so often we are convinced they are okay. Our heads are so full of our own racket, we don't even realize the implied messages in our words.

Now . . . let's get back to the helicopter pad.

What was the implied message when Lisa's parents were afraid to leave her with a baby-sitter? What's the implied message of calling a teacher to find friends for your son and setting up an overnighter?

The implied message of helicopter parenting is this: You are helpless. You need me to protect you, to do things for you, and to rescue you.

And when children hear this powerful, yet silent, message from us often enough, they begin to believe it.

Did you ever watch the grass beneath a hovering helicopter? The gale from the blades flattens the grass. The nickname for helicopter is also revealing—chopper.

Helicopters have their place in life—they are wonderful for rescue missions, medical emergencies, and battle fields.

But I'm not sure I want one in my family room.

Barking Orders

Drill sergeants make a lot of noise and racket, too. And drill sergeants bark out commands.

Drill sergeant parents are easily recognized even in profile. They're the ones with the jutting jaws, ramrod spines, and admonishing index fingers. They're also known by the familiar word sequence, "I don't care how you feel. I want it done, and I want it done NOW!"

I know those words well. Growing up, I did a lot of saluting to them. When my father said those words, I jumped up and did it—whatever it was—right then. I swore I was never going to be like him.

I've already told you about my first words in the classroom. "I don't care how you feel. I want it done now."

I said the same words as a parent. I had sworn I would never be a drill sergeant like my dad, and starting out, I succeeded. I was a really good helicopter instead.

However, when I was stressed, strained, or running on automatic with my children, every time I opened my mouth, my dad popped out.

At our house, bedtime often brought out the drill sergeant in me, and I barked, "You guys, get in that bed and go to sleep, now!"

Given a dollar for every time I said that, I'd be retired on my own island in the Bahamas. I invested more energy in ordering kids to sleep than I care to remember.

Demanding sleep never worked.

They giggled.

They wrestled.

They craved water.

They made bathroom trips.

They needed more water.

They saw monsters.

They remembered unfinished homework . . .

With each delay, my back got more straight, my tone got more stern, my voice got louder, my threats got harsher . . . and I never succeeded in producing sleep on demand.

I did succeed at making a lot of racket, though. Like helicopters, drill sergeants are also good at racket.

When Johnny comes home drooping and announces he doesn't have any friends, a drill sergeant makes a racket just as loud as a helicopter does. But it's a different kind of racket. It sounds like this:

"No friends? What did I tell you about friends? Are you being a good friend so the kids want to be friends with you?"

Johnny hesitates. "Aw, Dad, it isn't that big a deal. They just don't pick me for the ball team so much."

"That's the problem. Remember what I told you last spring at Little League time? I told you to sign up. I said, 'You get some coaching, some training. You get some skills and the kids will choose you to play with them.' Now we'll have to go out in the yard every night and practice. I have better things to do with my time, especially when it could have been done during Little League. But I'll find some way to get it done."

(The racket stops while Dad inhales, and then the barrage continues.)

"Come to think of it, I haven't seen many kids around so you can show them what a good friend you can be. You pick out three kids, tell them we're having an overnighter this weekend, and we'll get this thing straightened out."

Johnny tries again, "Dad . . . I . . . uh, I was hoping we'd do something quiet this weekend, like fixing my bike."

Dad's volume goes up a notch, his back gets a little more straight, and his index finger waggles skyward. "Well, there you have it. You're antisocial. I don't know how I can help you if you don't want to help yourself."

As with the helicopter, underneath the drill sergeant racket is an unspoken and powerful message:

I am more powerful than you. You can't think for yourself. I need to tell you what to do.

Here are some words drill sergeants use that send their message of power.

"Shut up!"

"Sit down!"

"Keep your hands to yourself."

"Sit up straight."

"What I say goes."

Sometimes drill sergeants add threats to orders. "You quiet down in that back seat, or I'm throwing you out of the car right here."

"Get your work done now, or you're not getting any dinner."

With or without threats, each of these orders says, "I'll overpower you. I'll make you do what I say."

Orders and threats eventually result in battle. To understand how that happens, we need to break ranks and leave our drill sergeant for a moment to look at control, power struggles, and threats.

A major issue between children and adults is the issue of power. I've discovered in working with kids that the more power I use, the more they make me use.

While still quite young, some kids realize they don't have much control over anything. The power struggle begins.

A child says to herself, "Oh, no—no control! I'm the smallest. They tell me what to do, they push me around, and I never get to make any decisions."

Suddenly, in her subconscious, a light goes on.

When the child sees that light, she realizes, "No control over my life? It doesn't matter. I can do better, anyway. I can control adults! I can control the color of Mom's face and the volume of Dad's voice."

As she gets older, at school, she thinks, "I can control whether the teacher teaches or whether she pays attention to my problems. I can feel powerful."

A child soon discovers there are certain battles adults can never win.

If he or she can hook an adult into these battles, he or she will burn up all of the adult's energy.

The adult won't have energy left for the battles he or she could have won. You see, there are some battles parents can win, and other battles they can't.

Battles adults can't win are battles for control of a child's brain activity.

If children hook adults into trying to make them talk, think, learn, or sleep they've got them.

Adults will never win those battles with kids.

However, there are ways adults can avoid battles with kids.

One way adults win is by using words which force the child to think, and let the child know when he or she may do something: "Those who have their rooms cleaned by Saturday morning will be going to the baseball game."

Another way adults win is when they describe the conditions under which they will do or allow something: "I'll be glad to listen when there's no whining."

Finally, adults also win when they provide children with opportunities to make choices: "My car is leaving at 7:30. If you're not ready I'll know you've chosen to walk to school." Or, "Chores need to be done by 5 p.m. Saturday. You may do them yourself or use your allowance to hire someone to do them for you."

When an old friend of mine heard me ordering my children to sleep, he asked me, "Jim, have you ever mastered the art of putting yourself to sleep?"

I hadn't.

"Then why do you think you can put other people to sleep? The more you yell, the more it keeps people awake!"

I mulled over his comment, and it changed my life. I realized that I had been in a power struggle with my kids over when they went to sleep.

That night my wife and I told our son Charlie, "We've been wrong. We're sorry."

"We will never again tell you when to go to sleep. That's your decision. Stay up all night if you like."

"There are only two rules you need to remember. Rule One: In our house, we get up every morning at 6:00."

"Rule Two: At 8:00 each evening, Mom and Dad's time alone begins. We don't want to see you or hear you, but feel free to stay awake in your room as late as you want."

We figured that battles over wake-up time and where he'd spend his late evenings were battles we could win.

The lights burned late in his room that night. In fact, they burned all night.

The next morning we found Charlie asleep, fully clothed, on the floor in the corner of his room with his baseball cap smashed down over his eyes.

But we learned that morning that my friend was right. We had been wasting our energy. It took only a few ergs of energy to joke and laugh loudly, practice my trombone, set three radios blaring and start the washing machine near his room.

Charlie woke up with a start.

That morning he staggered out of his room moaning, "I'm too tired. I can't go to school."

We empathized. "That's tough. It's no fun to get up tired. Hope the school day doesn't seem too terribly long for you." We hugged him and kissed him good-bye before he trudged to the bus.

At 4:00 that afternoon when the bus pulled up, we watched six-year-old Charlie stagger into the house and into bed.

He fell asleep with his coat and boots on. He didn't even take time to get his baseball hat off.

I hadn't quite learned, yet, the lesson of letting children make choices, so at 6:00 p.m. I woke Charlie for dinner, sure that he'd be hungry. He kept nodding off into his plate.

Before that meal ended, in a quiet, squeaky voice he said the most intelligent thing I had ever heard him say, "I think I'll go to bed early."

I thought, "Only one late night, and he learned. He finally learned."

When did Charlie learn? He learned when I picked a battle I knew I could win, and when I zipped my lip and let him think for himself.

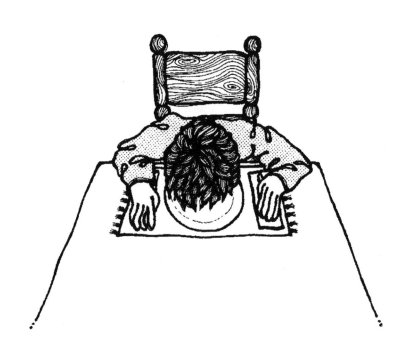

When I was ordering him to sleep, he spent more time being angry with me than thinking for himself. When I stopped the orders and threats, he experienced the consequences of making a poor decision and learned to turn his energy to solving his own problem.

Let's look for a moment at what happens when we use threats.

As a teacher I also often found myself using threats. After many years, I understand why.

I felt better about myself when I threatened than when I whimpered, begged, or pleaded.

I also got positive reinforcement on the few occasions when my threats worked.

In the classroom if Jolene didn't want to finish an assignment, I threatened, "You finish that work sheet, or you're not going to lunch."

Jolene completed the work sheet.

Then I went to Jason, whose worksheet was also half-done, and I repeated, "You're not going to lunch unless you finish the assignment."

But Jason said, "Who cares?"

I discovered that threats work with some people and not with others. Let's look at why threats don't work with many people.

When someone threatens me, the first thing I say to myself is, "He can't make me do that."

The second thing I say is, "But maybe he can."

An internal dialogue begins.

"No, he can't."

"Yes, he can."

"No, he can't."

"Yes, he can."

Soon the dialogue is an argument.

"NO, HE CAN'T!"

"YES, HE CAN!"

I get angry. I become resentful. I activate my passive-aggressive or my passive-resistive mode.

I'm acting passive-aggressively if, when you do something to me I don't like, I hurt you back—but I do it so subtly you don't even realize it's revenge.

And, you hurt enough that you think twice before asking me to do it again.

As a kid, when my teacher ordered me to work, I grabbed my paper and wrote down one word. Then I raised my hand to summon the teacher and asked, "Is this okay?"

She answered, "Jimmy, that's only one word. I'm not playing your game. You get to work!"

I waited until she was near her desk, wrote another word, and raised my hand again. She repeated her response. "Two words? Get to work. No more games."

I waited until she was seated. I walked to her desk with one sentence. "Is this all right? I really don't know what I'm supposed to do. My mom says good teachers make sure a kid knows what he's doing before they give assignments."

My purpose? To hurt her feelings so she'd think twice about making me work.

Perhaps at home you've experienced passive-aggressive dish washing when you've said, "I want those dishes washed. I'm tired of hearing you whining about it. Do it now!"

Your child says, "I'll do it. I'll do it!"

Then she "accidentally" breaks a piece of your good crystal.

What's the message? "You'd better think twice before you make me do dishes again!"

Occasionally passive-aggressive behavior goes undetected at the time, as one family learned at their family reunion.

The sons, now 27 and 34, asked their dad what he was doing for fun. He told them he was taking a course on working with children. He started telling them about how punishment gives a child a chance to focus his anger on somebody else instead of on his need to make changes.

That sparked a memory.

The younger son asked, "Do you remember when we were younger, and you were laid back about punishing? Mom used to tell you that you didn't care enough about us and that you should do more of the punishing? One day she got so mad because you hadn't punished me that she made you get out of the tub, dry off, and spank me before you finished your bath. Remember that?"

Dad remembered.

The son continued, "You took me into the bathroom and spanked me. Then you left me there to think about what I had done. Remember?"

Dad remembered.

"Well, Dad, I did some thinking, all right. And after considering things very carefully—I peed in your bath water!"

Passive-resistive behavior isn't aggressive. There's no pee in the bath water. I'm acting passive-resistively when I resist without letting you know I'm resisting you.

I was passive-resistive in school hallways. My teacher told me, "Jimmy, get down the hall, and get down there now."

I would walk so slowly she needed to compare me to a stationary object to see if I was making progress.

"Jimmy, hurry up! Don't dawdle."

I would respond, drawling slowly of course, "Now wait a minute. I'm doing what you told me. Why do you always hassle me? I'm doing what you said."

A passive-resistive child may realize eventually that adults can make him do things, but he holds the ultimate weapon. He realizes, "I'll do it, but not their way."

"If you make me do an assignment, I'll turn it in sloppy . . . "

" . . . Or I'll leave it half finished."

" . . . Or I'll reverse a lot of letters."

In resistance, the child regains a little control.

I wonder how many children in learning disabled classes are simply into resisting threats. It's hard to estimate, but I would guess about half of the children in those classes are just into saying, "You can maybe make me do it, but never your way."

When a drill sergeant begins to get into the threat mode, he doesn't realize it, but he may be triggering a war zone of passive-aggressive and passive-resistive responses.

But, drill sergeants have their place in the world.

When a military officer tells the troops to storm the bunker on the next hill, I wouldn't want some private saying, "Just a minute, Sarge, we first gotta take a vote on that."

Yes, drill sergeants have their place.

But I don't want one in my living room.

Zipped Lips and Magic

Consultants are always available to give suggestions and offer options. They also know when to zip their lips and let their clients make the final decision.

Consultant parents know how to zip their lips, too. They are willing to share alternative solutions to problems. They are willing to describe how they would solve the problem—if it were their problem.

Then consultant parents say, "It's your life. You get to decide. Good luck!"

And then they zip their lip.

The hardest job in parenting is zipping the lip. That's why we have helicopters and drill sergeants in homes. It's easier to make a racket than to zip our lips.

One crucial difference between consultant parents and helicopters or drill sergeants is ownership of a problem. Helicopters and drill sergeants both claim ownership of a child's problem. Consultant parents let the child retain ownership.

When Johnny droops over the kitchen table of a consultant parent and announces he's friendless, a consultant parent responds, "No friends! Hey, that's sad for you. What do you think you are going to do about it?"

When Johnny shrugs his shoulders, Mom says, "You don't know? That's even sadder—having a big problem and not knowing what you are going to do about it."

"I've watched other people with problems like that, and I could share with you some of the things they've tried. It might give you some ideas. If you ever want to hear what they tried, let me know . . . I sure hope you can work it out."

Then she zips her lip—until Johnny asks to hear what others have tried.

Allowing a child to keep ownership of a problem sends an implied message, too. That message is: "You are wise enough to make good decisions. I trust you to know how to handle this."

That implied message builds a child up instead of putting him down.

When I quit using implied messages to put kids down, they quit using guerrilla warfare. They quit sabotaging me and shooting me down at home and in the classroom.

When I started using implied messages that built kids up, the quality of my life went up. At home my kids reacted in a much more loving way, and students became much easier to work with at school.

Magically, giving a child choices and ownership of his or her decisions also gives an adult more control.

That control was desperately needed by two parents I saw one day at Burger Heaven. I walked in just as they were finishing their meal. They were ready to go, and I could see that they were getting anxious.

However, their little girl had taken just one bite from her hamburger and had eaten about two french fries.

Mom, whose face was starting to flush, said, "All right, hurry up with that thing. We don't have all night. We've got some shopping to do."

Then Dad got into the act, snapping, "Can't you do something with that kid? Save-Mart will be closed by the time we get out of here."

There was still no response from their daughter.

The next time I glanced over, the mother had the hamburger in her hand and in desperation she was guiding it into her daughter's face.

Then the threats started. "Okay, you hurry up or we're going to just go and leave you here."

Still no response from the child.

Dad jumped up from his chair and said, "Okay, that does it. We're going to leave you here, and the cops are going to come and get you."

When I left Burger Heaven, the little girl still had half her hamburger and fries on her plate, and her parents were still working on her. I don't think they ever made it to Save-Mart.

When a child dawdles over a burger and fries and her parents are eager to shop, they can scold, they can threaten—or they can let the child own the problem and the decision.

A parent who would give a child credit for being able to make his or her own decisions is also a parent who uses my favorite phrase, "No problem."

Children can translate that phrase in a hurry. It means, "No problem for the adult, big problem for the kid!"

This type of parent would say to his daughter in Burger Heaven, "No problem. My car is leaving in five minutes. There are two ways to leave with me. Hungry is one way. Not hungry is the other way. You decide."

A child who has *no* control over his or her life is a child who will spend nearly one hundred percent of his or her time trying to take control of adults and manipulate the system. A child who has *some* control over his or her life will spend very little time trying to control adults or manipulate the system. It's like magic!

Offering alternatives as a way of keeping the control you need works with adults, too—including me.

Over the years I'd developed a way to avoid speeding tickets. I acted like an absentminded old dude who was really happy to have been stopped or otherwise probably would have killed himself driving so fast.

It worked. In the past decade I'd gotten plenty of warning tickets, and I had the act down to an art.

Then, en route to Florida, I was stopped by a Texas State Trooper. He treated me the same way I teach parents and teachers to treat children—with Love and Logic.

As he approached me with a smile and a handshake, he said, "Wow, Colorado license plates. I'll bet you're on a trip."

I said, "Yes, I'm on my way to Florida to visit my kids."

And he said, "Oh, I can understand, then, that you're probably anxious to get there, and that's why you were going so fast. Well, let me tell you why I stopped you."

"The radar said 73 miles per hour, and in this state any time someone is up to that speed, I'm not allowed to do anything but write you a citation."

"Don't feel bad, though. You don't have to go back to the county seat and deal with it right now, if you don't want to. You have several other choices. I'll give you this letter, which outlines them."

"You can, for instance, just mail in your fine."

"Or you can contest the ticket. A lot of people like to do that, and this letter tells you how, if that's what you decide."

Then the trooper put out his hand, smiled, and said, "Have a good trip now."

"Thank you," I automatically said.

As I sat in my car, shaking my head, I said to my wife, Shirley, "I can't believe what I just did. I just thanked that cop for this ticket!"

That Texas State Trooper had put my own moves on me so fast that I couldn't put any moves on him. He had my head swimming, trying to decide between going back to the county seat, paying the ticket by mail, or contesting it.
I didn't have any time or brainpower to argue. All I could muster was, "Thank you."

When we follow that Texas State Trooper's example, we prevent the threats from ever getting started. Instead, we give choices and share the decision-making.

5

**Self-care, Options, and Action—
Three Rules for Consultant Parenting**

If you'd like to try being a consultant parent, I suggest you follow three rules:

Rule 1: Take good care of yourself.

Rule 2: Provide your child with choices you can live with.

Rule 3: Take action.

Used regularly, these three simple rules can prevent power struggles and silence the racket of helicopters and drill sergeants.

When you take good care of yourself, you roll your bowling ball with a child-free arm. You gently inform your child of what you are going to do, rather than ordering him to do something. You model for your child how taking good care of oneself is done.

When you provide options and alternatives, children use their energy to control their own lives. They use their brains to weigh their choices. And they are too busy thinking to argue with you.

When you take action, you allow natural consequences to fall. Consultant parents don't protect their children from making mistakes. They allow their child to make decisions, and then they stand back and hope and pray that the child makes a poor decision so that he or she can learn from the natural consequences of that decision. Taking action does NOT mean protecting children from bad choices, or rescuing them from the consequences of their mistakes!

Let's meet some parents who are living by these three rules. Sometimes they are using only one of the rules, and sometimes they're using all three.

Let's peek first through a kitchen window where Mom has spent an afternoon preparing a family feast.

Erica comes to the table and sees food on her plate she's never seen before—chicken cacciatore.

Does she say, "Wow, I bet you worked hard on that, Mom. You must feel proud!"?

No way! She uses the three-letter word many kids say when they see a foreign food on their plate. She says, "YUK!"

Mom has three choices.

Helicopter: "Aw, that's not very nice. I spent all afternoon slaving over a hot stove. Come on, try a bite. You'll like it."

Drill Sergeant: "You eat that food and you eat it now! You're not leaving the table until you do!"

Consultant: Zip the lip and take action.

This mom's a consultant. She gently says, "No, problem," and she takes the plate and puts the food away.

She continues softly, "Run along. Do what kids do after dinner. We'll see you at breakfast."

Later that evening Erica returns to the kitchen. "I'm hungry!"

Mom says, "For sure, Erica. But don't worry, we'll have a nice big breakfast tomorrow morning."

Let's look in on another family. Brian, age 5, knows he has a bucketful of power. He can make his mother late for work.

Mom has tried the standard stuff. She's tried begging, pleading, and nagging. She's tried scolding, popping him on the rear, and taking things away from him. This morning she tries consulting. She gives him options and a little control. And she takes care of herself—she tells him what she is going to do.

"Brian," she says, "I'm so excited. Starting today, I'll never be late for work again, because my car leaves at 7:30, and I'll get there on time. There are two ways you can go with me. Would you like to hear what they are?"

Brian says, puzzled, "I guess so."

Mom says, "Dressed is one way and not dressed is another."

She shows him what 7:30 looks like on the clock, and she heads for her bedroom.

At 7:30 Brian's not ready. Mom says, "No problem. You probably didn't feel like dressing. I have a nice box here for your clothes. You can dress whenever you feel like it."

She puts the box under her arm, takes him by the hand, and out they go. As she starts the car, she says, "I'm really glad I'm going to get to work on time."

Brian's got some spunk and he goes for the jugular. "You don't love me. You put me in the back seat with my pajamas on."

He hauls out his arsenal.

He jumps up and down.

He kicks the back of the front seat.

He waves to passing motorists like he's being kidnapped.

But soon Mom hears a rustle of fabric in the back seat, and a small voice says, "Guess I better be dressed by 7:30 after this."

In another car, three unruly teenage boys in the back seat are engaged in World War III.

A drill sergeant Dad would threaten, "You guys shut up back there, or I'm throwing you out of the car."

A helicopter parent would whimper, "Can't you guys be good back there after all I've done for you? I can't drive with that fighting. If you don't stop, I'll have an accident."

But this Dad's a consultant. He says, just once, "Hey, guys, I'd like it quiet back there."

It doesn't happen.

Dad takes action.

He pulls over to the curb, gets out, opens the back door, and says, "Well, here we are."

The kids get out of the car asking, "What do you mean, 'Here we are'? We're still six blocks from home."

Dad gets back in, locks the doors, and says, "It's going to be fun driving home without my ears being hassled. See you there!"

Dad takes care of himself and peacefully drives back home.

A friend of mine tried this technique. But when she opened the car door, she was staring at 400 pounds of teenagers with their arms crossed and their legs locked.

"You've got to be kidding," they said. "We're not leaving this car."

Mom thought fast. "I asked you in a nice way, and you're not getting out?"

"Nope. You can't make us."

They were right.

Mom said, "I need to think this over. I'm going to get a cup of coffee while I think about it."

While the confused teens stared at her, Mom walked over to a restaurant across the street.

Ten minutes later the kids watched a cab pull up to the front of the restaurant. Mom got in and rode off.

She smiled and waved as she passed her parked car.

When the teenagers reached home—on foot—they didn't say one word about the incident.

It's been a year since it happened, and they still haven't said anything.

Their mom says there's been a dramatic shift in their behavior, though. They treat her with a lot more respect.

Letting the kids walk isn't possible if you're too far from home, the roads are too busy, or the kids are too young.

Other friends of mine found a different solution on a busy highway in Chicago. Dad pulled off onto the shoulder as far as he could. He and Mom got out of the car without a word, walked up a little knoll, and sat down on the grass. They relaxed, pointed at scenery, smiled, and appeared to be really enjoying themselves.

Soon, from the car, they heard a desperate conversation.

"Shut up, or they're never coming back here."

"You better be quiet, or we'll never get there."

When the car was quiet, Mom and Dad got back in and drove off.

Half an hour later, it was a little loud in the back seat again; however, it was still within reasonable range.

By coincidence, though, Dad needed to make a quick switch into the right lane.

From the back seat the parents heard a frantic whisper, "Shut up! Here we go again!"

Let's look at one more consultant parent. It's time to divide up the chores. Ten-year-old Tim is eating his after-school granola bar, and his mom says, "You can bring in the wood when you wish, but it needs to be in by the end of the day, Tim. That means when I go to bed tonight I can know that everything is finished up around the house. Got it?"

"Got it," says Tim.

The assignment provides Tim with lots of choices. He can watch TV or bring in the wood. When his favorite show is over, he can play or go get the wood.

On her way to bed Tim's mom stops at his room, where he's already asleep. She wakes him up saying, "Hey, Tim, guess what? It's the end of the day and the wood hasn't been brought in."

"I know it's hard to wake up once you've fallen asleep, so I brought this nice cold washcloth to help. If you want to put it on your forehead, you can. I'll even help you so you don't stumble on the stairs on your way outside."

After Tim has brought in the wood, Mom says, "Now the day is complete. I know that everything is finished and I can go to bed. Thanks. See you in the morning."

By Mom's taking action, Tim learns from the consequences.

My mother used these same techniques in training me. On my junior high graduation day I asked her to iron my dress pants which I had rolled up and thrown into a bottom drawer. She said, "Sorry, Jim. I used up that time this week doing the dishes you forgot to do."

"Mom," I said. "This is important! What am I going to do?"

"You could wear them wrinkled, or you could try ironing them yourself," she said.

I tried ironing—and created an iron-shaped hole in the right knee. "Now what will I do?" I asked.

"Well, Jim, I suppose you could wear them, or stay home, or wear your jeans," she said.

I wore my jeans. Whenever I think of my junior high graduation, my face still flushes with embarrassment.

Conclusion

Children raised by consultant parents grow up to be adults who:
- know how to respect and take care of themselves
- are able to determine who owns the problem
- know that they have some control over their lives
- know that you gain control by giving away the control you don't need
- know that the quality of their lives depends upon the decisions they make

If the choice were mine today, I'd give consultant parenting a try. The quality of my life improved when I tried it.

But the choice is really yours. Good luck with your decision. Hope it works out well for you and your family.

The Author

Jim Fay, with over 30 years experience in education, is one of America's most sought-after presenters and consultants. Jim's "Love and Logic" philosophy has revolutionized the way parents and professionals work with children. He is the author of over 90 books, tapes and articles on parenting and positive discipline.

Call today for a free catalog of our complete line of Love and Logic books and audio and video tapes.

1-800-338-4065